For
Grandpa
FRom
TeDDy 1896

GOLF TALK

Compiled by
Laurence Beilenson

Illustration by
Abigail L. Adams

PETER PAUPER PRESS, INC.

WHITE PLAINS, NEW YORK

For John and Wanda

Copyright © 1996
Peter Pauper Press, Inc.
202 Mamaroneck Avenue
White Plains, NY 10601
ISBN 0-88088-796-6
Printed in Hong Kong
7 6 5 4 3 2 1

GOLF TALK

Introduction

Golf is a game the aim of which is to hit a small ball into an even smaller hole with weapons singularly ill-designed for the purpose.

Sir Winston Churchill

Mr. Churchill is eloquent, not to mention downright accurate, in this description of the game. What, then, accounts for the

unprecedented popularity of the sport nearly half a century later? It is to be hoped that this collection of thoughts from touring professionals past and present can lend some insight to the question. But we doubt it!

Then again, Churchill never did have an oversize driver. . . .

L. B.

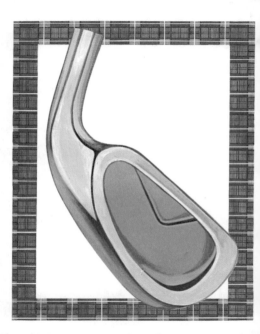

If you are caught on a golf course during a storm and are afraid of lightning, hold up a 1-iron. Not even God can hit a 1-iron.

Lee Trevino

[Jack Nicklaus is] a legend in
his spare time.

Chi Chi Rodriguez

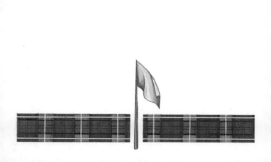

In eighteen years of tournament golf I feel that I've never tried a shot that I couldn't make.

Arnold Palmer

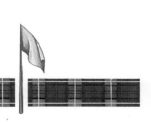

The Temptation is there. It's a
bit like alcohol: reach for the
driver, reach for a beer. I tell
myself not to do it.

John Daly,
*on being tempted to use
his driver on tight courses*

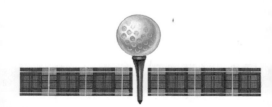

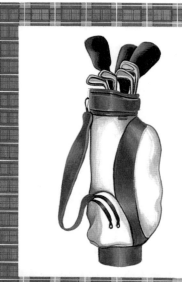

The woods are full of long drivers.

Harvey Penick

I've known the agony and the ecstasy. I'm convinced I've got more of both ahead of me.

Greg Norman

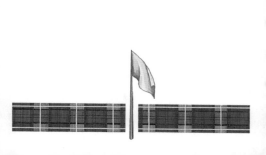

Forget your opponents; always play against par.

Sam Snead

Golf is the most fun you can have without taking your clothes off.

Chi Chi Rodriguez

The last time I had this much
fun was a root-canal operation.

Larry Ziegler

Golf isn't just my business, it's
my hobby.

Lee Trevino

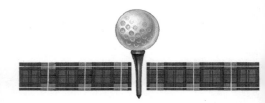

I think it was supposedly attributed to Confucius and he said something like, "The man who finds a job that he truly loves never works another day the rest of his life." I have a job that I truly love. I don't feel like I work at that game. If you want to call me a playaholic, then let's do that.

Tom Kite

It felt like you were swinging a baseball bat with boxing gloves on. But just because you're nervous doesn't mean you can't do it.

Paul Azinger,
about Ryder Cup competition

I accept the fact that I'm going
to miss it sometimes. I just
hope I miss it where I can
find it.

Fuzzy Zoeller

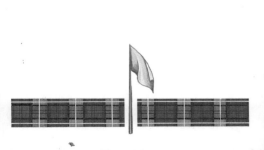

I do know the money means
absolutely nothing. Just to be
able to go out there and win
golf tournaments, that's the
whole deal.

Peter Jacobsen

I hit the wrong shot with the
wrong club at the wrong time.

Tom Watson,
explaining how he lost the
1984 British Open at St. Andrews

Swing easy and hit hard.
                                        Julius Boros

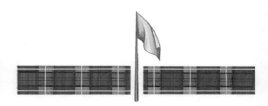

Nobody ever swung the golf
club too slowly.

Bobby Jones

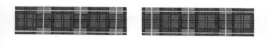

Keeping the head still is golf's one universal, unarguable fundamental.

Jack Nicklaus

What drives me to go to the practice tee is the same as it's always been. It's the quality of my golf—that's what keeps me going.

Nick Price

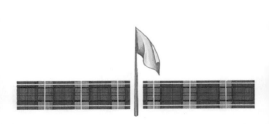

I just want to be a great player and I'm not even close. I'm not a superstar—Michael Jordan's a superstar. He can dominate every time he plays.

Fred Couples

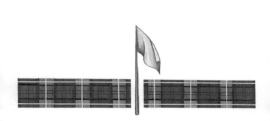

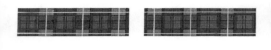

I wanna have more majors than Jack Nicklaus.

John Daly

I have found the game to be, in all factualness, a universal language wherever I traveled at home or abroad.

Ben Hogan

If you get a bunch of golfers
together, there isn't much talk
about golf, it's mostly fishing,
boats, houses, stereos, things
normal people talk about. If I
go home, there's hardly any.

Davis Love III

When the ducks are walking, you know it's too windy to play golf.

Dave Stockton

If I could have shot 69 in the last round every time, I would have won nine U.S. Opens. *Nine.*

Sam Snead

I'd rather hit an 8-iron from the rough than a 4-iron from the fairway.

JoAnne Carner

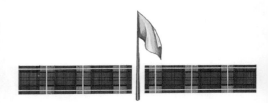

Golf courses are the Demaret answer to the world's problems. When I get out on that green carpet called a fairway and manage to poke the ball right down the middle, my surroundings look like a touch of heaven on earth.

Jimmy Demaret

It's good to get the monkey off my back about majors. But it was my own monkey that I'd put on my own back.

Corey Pavin

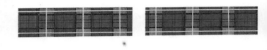

Son, I can poop one into the
water and it don't even splash.

Tommy Bolt

Man, I go rabbit hunting in that stuff [the rough]. You don't go in there; you send your beagle in there to get something out. . . . I'm lucky I didn't break any bones.

Fuzzy Zoeller

A fine golfer only has one fine thing—his fine golf game.

Byron Nelson, Jr.

This is the origin of the game,
golf in its purest form; and it's
still played that way on a course
seemingly untouched by time.
Every time I play here, it
reminds me that this is still
a game.

Arnold Palmer,
about the Old Course at St. Andrews

The reason the Road Hole [at
St. Andrews] is the hardest
par-4 in the world is because
it's a par-5.

Ben Crenshaw

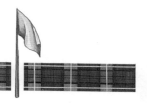

I entered my first tournament at age thirteen. . . . I entered as a 24 handicap, shot an 80 and was refunded my entry fee. I just got hot, but the officials weren't buying that.

Billy Casper

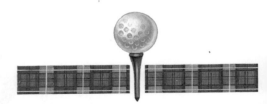

Forget the last shot. It takes so long to accept that you can't always replicate your swing. The only thing you can control is your attitude toward the next shot.

Mark McCumber

You're completely alone, with every conceivable opportunity to defeat yourself.

Hale Irwin

Your confidence is the 15th
club in your bag. You'd like it to
be a thick-headed driver . . .
But it sometimes seems like a
pretty weak little stick.

Peter Jacobsen

When you lip out several putts in a row, you should never think that means that you're putting well. . . . When you're putting well, the only question is what part of the hole it's going to fall in, not if it's going in.

Jack Nicklaus

All other things being equal,
greens break to the west.

Ben Hogan

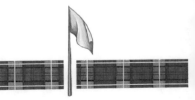

Every golfer scores better when
he learns his capabilities.

Tommy Armour

All I really need to know about
drugs is that you can't take
them and play golf.

Nancy Lopez

The pressure of golf can change you so you hardly know yourself. You have more electrical connections in your head than a whole city. You'll do anything to keep 'em from going blooey on you in the crunch. I have only one goal in golf—to leave it with my sanity.

Joe Inman

Putting affects the nerves more than anything. I would actually get nauseated over three-footers, and there were tournaments when I couldn't keep a meal down for four days.

Byron Nelson, Jr.

I'd like the demeanor of Couples, the patience of Faldo, the course management of Nicklaus, the imagination of Ballesteros, the short game of Watson, the putting of Crenshaw, the power of Norman.

Phil Mickelson

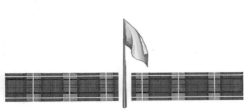

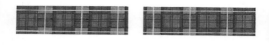

This [The Masters] is probably
the hardest tournament in the
world to win from the front.
Probably ninety percent win
from behind. . . . There's so
much pressure here. This course
asks for perfection.

Nick Faldo

Management is eighty percent
of winning golf.

Ben Hogan

I think we have arrived at the stage where we are making it too complicated. I know guys who can't play two rounds before running to their teachers.

Vijay Singh

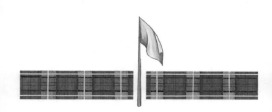

I've never seen [a sports psychologist] shake over a four-footer for a British Open or Masters title.

Lee Trevino

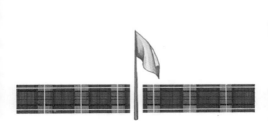

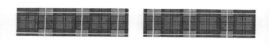

There is no truth in the idea
that the person who hits the
most balls will become the best
golfer. Golf is a bizarre sport.
You can work for years and
years on your game, without
making any improvement in
your score.

Fred Couples

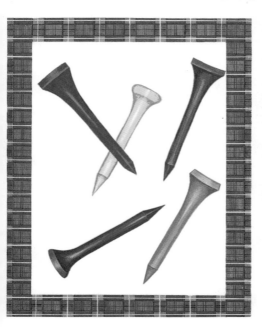

I don't want to be the best black golfer ever. I want to be the best *golfer* ever.

Tiger Woods

It's a good thing I don't carry a gun.

Scott Hoch,
*after missing a two-foot putt
to lose the 1989 Masters*

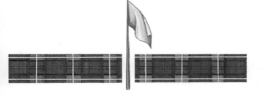

I never fought him, only his army.

Jack Nicklaus,
about Arnold Palmer

It may be monotonous, but I sure eat regular.

Byron Nelson, Jr.,
during his streak of 11 straight
victories in 1945

It's mass confusion. I'm guess-
ing on every shot. About the
only thing left for me is
acupuncture in the brain.

George Archer,
during a long slump

Golf is the hardest game in the world. There's no way you can ever get it. Just when you think you do, the game jumps up and puts you in your place.

Ben Crenshaw

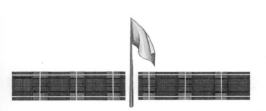

As athletes, we have been given a platform that gives us the ability to encourage people. I never really took advantage of that. It's amazing what a simple two-minute phone call to someone who is hurting will do.

Paul Azinger,

while undergoing chemotherapy treatment for cancer

The game embarrasses you
until you feel inadequate and
pathetic. You want to cry like
a child.

Ben Crenshaw

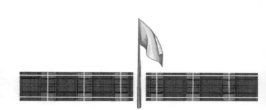

The best swing is the one that repeats. And that's what I have. . . . Years ago, I had a one-iron that I could hit 260 yards through a doorway. Now I can hit it through the keyhole.

Lee Trevino

The competitive level out here
[the Senior Tour] is fast reach-
ing that of the regular Tour—
and the money isn't terribly far
behind. In some cases the good
old days were never this good.

Billy Casper

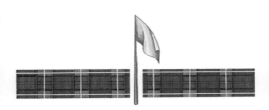

I enjoy playing the senior tournaments; it's kinda fun. But am
I really beating the best players
in the world? No, I'm living in
the past. I'm beating a bunch of
fellas that are my age.

Jack Nicklaus

I know you can get fined for throwing a club, but I want to know if you can get fined for throwing a caddie?

Tommy Bolt

Golf is the one game I know
which becomes more and more
difficult the longer one plays it.
Bobby Jones

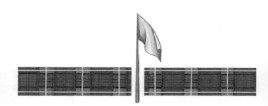

Well, here it is and from here I have to play it.

Walter Hagen,

*responding to a spectator after
his ball took a bad bounce*

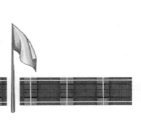

The press still considers me one of the most laid-back athletes since Babe Ruth. That's supposed to be a criticism, but I consider it a compliment because I think being carefree on the course is one of the secrets to scoring well consistently.

Fred Couples

I'd like to thank the press from
the bottom of my . . . well,
from the heart of my bottom,
anyway.

Nick Faldo

The perfect round of golf
would be an 18. I almost
dreamed it once. I had seven-
teen holes in one and lipped
out at the last. I was mad
as hell.

Ben Hogan

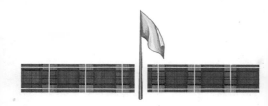